Duncan and Trevor Smith are son and father respectively and this is their third co-written book. Their previous works are the highly successful *South and West Yorkshire Curiosities* (1992) and *North and E*   *Curiosities* (1993), both published by The Dovecote Press. Together th   ~rous articles to the *Dalesman* magazine and have lectured '

Duncan Smith was born in Sheffield in   l
an avid collector of all things historical,   k
Archaeology at Birmingham University   e:
collector, he currently works in the publishing ...   :al
A Portrait in Colour (The Dovecote Press) which rec..   ing
acclaim. He is also proprietor of The Ridings Press which is commit...
reasonably priced local interest books with a broad appeal.

Trevor Smith of Scottish extraction, was born in Sheffield in 1921. He has had a varied career, including some eight years of teaching and many more in public and university libraries. He has a lifelong interest in freelance writing and photography and for some considerable time has been compiling a list of curiosities of the British Isles. His other interests include military history and English and American literature.

Other books published by The Ridings Press:
Cycling Around South Yorkshire, Arnold Robinson (1995)
Peak District Tales For Young and Old, Peter J. Marsden-Fereday (1995)

Overleaf: A combined civic drinking fountain and street lamp on Broad Lane inscribed in Latin "With God helping, work will progress", words also found below the city crest.

SHEFFIELD CURIOSITIES

Duncan and Trevor Smith

 *The Ridings Press*

Queen Victoria's Diamond Jubilee Obelisk, Endcliffe Park (See no. 42)

Photo credits: Duncan Smith / The Ridings Press (all photos);
except Simon Laffoley (nos. 30, 33, 48, 50); Trevor Smith (nos. 18, 19).

First published in 1997 by
The Ridings Press, 62 Sheldon Road, Sheffield, South Yorkshire S7 1GX

ISBN 0 9527235 2 2

© Duncan and Trevor Smith 1997

Typeset by Commercial Services
Carnson House, 1 Moorgate Road, Rotherham S60 2EE
Printed and bound in Doncaster

INTRODUCTION

Sheffield is England's fourth largest city and as such can boast a rich history stretching far back into the past. Although it is short on prehistoric remains, and was bypassed by the Romans, its suburb of Dore played a part in Anglo-Saxon history, and Sheffield itself still has the remains of a Norman castle below its market. The Middle Ages saw a thriving town on the banks of the Sheaf and Don from which several half-timbered buildings remain. All was to change during the eighteenth and nineteenth century Industrial Revolution when Sheffield began to utilise fully its enviable supply of clay, coal, iron, and fast flowing streams. The city became the world's greatest producer of steel, turning out everything from knives and forks, to railway axles and plates for the hulls of Dreadnought battleships. Sheffield cutlery adorned tables around the globe and much still remains from this period.

The Second World War brought great devastation as the city was earmarked for heavy enemy bombing and many fine Victorian and Edwardian buildings were lost. With the large scale rebuilding that followed, and the collapse of the heavy steel industry in the 1970's, Sheffield reinvented itself as a centre for tourism, leisure, service industries and special steels.

The aim of this book is to trawl this rich and chequered heritage for tangible remains of Sheffield's bygone days. These survivals, or 'curiosities', can be as modest as milestones and street lamps, or as obvious as monuments and listed buildings. What connects them all is that each has a story to tell and a part to play in the historical development of a great city.

Duncan and Trevor Smith, Sheffield, 1997

CONTENTS

MAP SHOWING THE LOCATION OF
SHEFFIELD CURIOSITIES

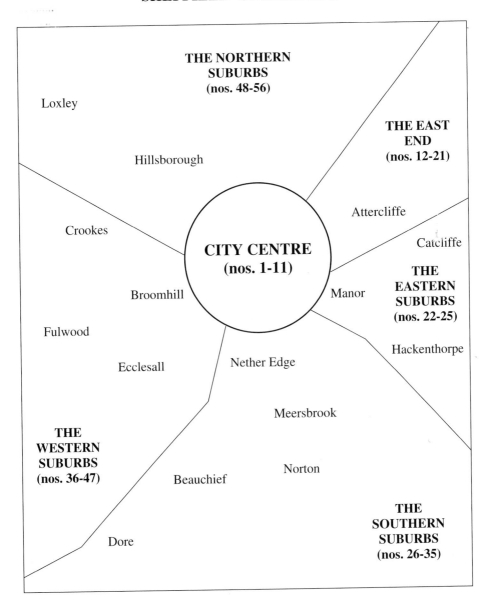

(The authors recommend that a detailed Sheffield Street plan is used to pinpoint curiosities when visiting. For maps showing bygone Sheffield, the Alan Godfrey series of old Ordnance Survey maps is fascinating.)

1. The Doctor Who Box

SURREY STREET, S1

Outside the Town Hall on the corner of Surrey Street is an old-fashioned police box, the last of 120 which once dotted the city. Today it is no longer in its original blue livery and lacks its blue light which flashed when an urgent telephone call came through. An example at the Crich Tramway Museum still retains these classic features. Such police boxes were introduced to Sheffield in 1928 by Chief Constable Percy J. Sillitoe, of gang-busting fame, and not phased out until the 1960's. They were also used by patrolmen for meal breaks and writing reports.

Around the corner on Norfolk Street at the Halifax Building Society is a doorway inscribed "The Jeffie Bainbridge Children's Shelter" where food and shelter awaited waifs and strays. It was erected to his wife's memory by Emerson Bainbridge, a well-known philanthropist and Justice of the Peace, and opened in 1894 by the Duchess of Portland.

2. Measure for Measure

ST. PAUL'S PARADE, S1

Along one side of St. Paul's Parade is a 100 foot long stone parapet studded with brass knobs and inscribed at various intervals. A plaque tells us it is the "City of Sheffield Standard Measures of length presented to the city by the Rt. Hon. the Lord Mayor (the Earl Fitzwilliam, DSO) and by him declared available for public use on the occasion of the visit of the British Association, September 1910". This unusual example of public education was installed by Troughton and Simms of London and shows pre-metric measurement, such as chains, links and poles, which seem archiac to us today.

The adjacent Peace Gardens, named after Chamberlain's "Peace in our Time" pledge, once held the old St. Paul's church, pieces of which can be seen in houses on Trap Lane at Bents Green. The fountain below the Town Hall Extension is dedicated to Samuel Holberry (1814-42), Sheffield's Chartist leader who died in York Castle. There is also a bell donated by the people of Bochum in 1986 to mark the 35 years since the two cities were twinned.

3. A Clock Jack and Plaque
ORCHARD SQUARE, S1

The Orchard Square shopping complex opened in 1987 and, being in a conservation area opposite the Town Hall, its architecture is in keeping with some of Sheffield's older buildings. In the square itself is a clock tower where, on the hour, figures of a buffer girl and grinder appear much to the delight of onlookers. Below this 'clockjack', as such apparatus is called, is a plaque to the memory of John Brown (1816-1896), inventor of the conical spring railway buffer and pioneer manufacturer of railway lines and armour plate. He was born here in what was then Favell's Yard, and worked as an apprentice in nearby Orchard Place, setting up his first steelmaking workshop in 1844 at 24 Orchard Street. Other shops which once occupied the Square include the Sheffield Creamery Co., the Atlas Printing Works and the Fleur de Lys Pub where servicemen in the Second World War could get a meal for 6d.

4. A Beastly Building

FARGATE, S1

If, whilst walking down Fargate one gazes up at the facade of the W.H. Smith building, four carved heads of pigs and cows will be seen. They have no connection whatsoever with the present shop, rather they were part of the original design of 1882 for Arthur Davy and Sons Ltd., who operated a pork butchers and general grocers store here. Older citizens may still remember when the upper storeys contained Davy's well-known cafe-restaurant. Further down Fargate the facade of the telephone shop bears carved books and quills reminding us that this was once a book shop.

Opposite, at number 10 Norfolk Row, is a plaque marking the spot where, on the evening of 22nd March 1889, the Committee of Sheffield United Cricket Club met with senior officials from the Sheffield Football Association in the office of club secretary John Wostinholm and decided to form a new football club for the 1889-90 season. Next day an advertisement in the Sheffield Morning Newspapers invited professional players to send testimonials to Wostinholm and Sheffield United was born.

5. Where Trams Once Ran

THE MOOR, S1

On October 6th, 1873, the first horse-drawn tram clip-clopped from Lady's Bridge to the Golden Ball, Attercliffe heralding a tram system which went on to cover most of the city until its closure on October 8th, 1960. In 1896 the Corporation took over the Sheffield Tramways Co. and by 1899 had opened the first electric route from Nether Edge to Tinsley. Over the next few decades the system encompassed most suburbs and stretched some 50 route miles. Many of the trams were built locally by Cravens of Darnall and the Corporation's own Queens Road works, their largely cream livery said to make them stand out and to encourage cleaning! Little remains of the trams today except for empty depots (see no. 20) and preserved trams at the Crich Tramway Museum in Derbyshire. However, occasionally road works reveal steel tram lines as was the case recently when the Moor was redeveloped. A section was preserved together with two brick-built trams (pictured) as a permanent reminder of one of the first, and last, tram systems in Britain.

6. Relish The Thought !

LEAVYGREAVE ROAD, S3

On Leavygreave Road are the modest premises where Sheffield's famous Henderson's Relish has been produced since 1960. The plain orange label, recommending it "for chops, steaks, soups, fish and game", and the no-nonsense bottle, conceal a Yorkshire delicacy which includes such exotic ingredients as tamarinds, cloves, garlic oil and cayenne pepper. Across the road is the original doorway of the "Jessop Hospital for Women", founded by Thomas Jessop in 1878 to replace the "Sheffield Women's Hospital" in Figtree Lane, founded in 1864.

Further down, in the corner of St. George's churchyard, is the tomb of Benjamin Coldwell of Upperthorpe, owner of the Nursery Lime and Plaster Works, who died in 1868. It befits a man whose personal library was open to the public that his grave should be inscribed with the words and music of his favourite hymn.

Finally, on Regent Street, is a plaque marking the home of Samuel Plimsoll (1824-98) who in 1876, devised the uniform loading line for ships (the 'Plimsoll line'). A new type of canvas shoe developed in the same year was named the 'plimsoll' in his honour.

7. Sewer Gas Lamps

ELDON STREET, S1

Eldon Street, off West Street, is one of 18 roads in Sheffield still adorned with a "J.E. Webb Patent Sewer Gas Destructor" lamp standard. Patented by J.E. Webb & Co., Birmingham in 1895 they burned town gas whilst also destroying foul and potentially explosive methane gas from the sewers below. 84 were erected in Sheffield between 1914 and 1935, the greatest number in any British town, due largely to the many hills where gases could be trapped. That so many still survive is due initially to the conserving efforts of a local postman and several children who counted them up in the 1960's. Others exist on Cemetery Road, Brincliffe Edge Road, London Road and Westbourne Road.

Returning to Eldon Street, it is hard to imagine that George Wostenholm's mighty Washington Works once stood near here until demolition in 1978. All that remains of the cutlery works is part of the name tablet built into the back wall of the Washington pub on Wellington Street.

8. Paradise in Sheffield?

PARADISE SQUARE, S1

Paradise Square certainly befits its name in terms of architectural splendour, being the finest Georgian ensemble in the city. It was built largely by banker Thomas Broadbent in 1771, his own home being the impressive Old Banker's House on Hartshead. His father had built the north side of the Square in 1739. Although it is occupied today by the legal and property professions, the old street lamps, cobbles and boot scrapes still lend an old-world charm. Once an open space where meetings and markets were held it was popular with preachers, notably John Wesley, founder of Methodism. He wrote in his journal on 15th July 1779, "I preached . . . to the largest congregation I ever saw on a week day". A plaque to Wesley was unveiled in 1951 by film magnate J. Arthur Rank. At number 24 is a plaque to sculptor Sir Francis Chantrey (see no. 31) who had a studio here, and at number 12 is another to physician David Daniel Davis who lived here (1803-1812) and assisted at the birth of Queen Victoria. He also translated Pinel's *'Treatise on Insanity'*.

9. Sheffield's Hidden Castle

EXCHANGE STREET, S1

The modern visitor would find little or no evidence that Sheffield once boasted one of the greatest castles in Northern England. However, behind a door at the back of the Castle Market are stairs leading down to a single lump of masonry – all that remains of the mighty fortress. The real story of Sheffield begins with the timber castle built by Baron William de Lovetot after the Norman Conquest in the twelfth century. It was situated at the junction of the Sheaf and Don which acted as a moat. The Normans built a church, town mill, hospital and market, and it is said their archers practised on the Wicker! Thomas de Furnival rebuilt the castle in stone in 1270 and the first market charter was granted in 1296. Mary Queen of Scots was held here (1570-84) by the Earl of Shrewsbury and in 1648 the castle was demolished as punishment for protecting the King's troops in the Civil War. Castle Market now occupies the site and only street names such as Fargate, Furnival Gate and Castlegate remind us of the days when the Saxon Manor of Hallam, which included Sheffield (Escafeld), came under the influence of the Normans.

10. From Ponds to Swimming Pools
SHEAF STREET, S1

Occupying much of Sheaf Street today is the ultra modern Ponds Forge international swimming baths and sports centre built in the early 1990's. Its Olympic length pool was used during the World Student Games and helped Sheffield become the 1996 National City of Sport. It is hard to believe that until 1988 the area was occupied by George Senior's vast iron foundry, the gateway to which, erected in 1900, has been re-built on Pond Hill. A water-powered forge driven by the River Sheaf existed here in 1736, being expanded in the 1770's and becoming steam-powered in 1805. In 1852 Marsh Brothers took over until the building of the Midland Railway Station caused the river to be diverted in 1870. George Senior took the works over in 1872. The only other reminder of the original Ponds Forge, named because of a spring close by, is an 80 ton steam-hammer anvil block outside the baths on Sheaf Street.

11. Sheffield's Oldest Pub

POND HILL, S1

Now surrounded entirely by modern structures and the busy Sheffield Interchange, the Old Queen's Head public house is the oldest house in central Sheffield. It was built in c. 1475 and is the last remnant of the timber-framed medieval town of Sheffield before it was rebuilt in brick and stone. Once known as "The Hawle in the Pondes" it would originally have been surrounded by riverside fields close to the track leading to the castle and Lady's Bridge. The building has also been referred to as the former wash-house to Sheffield manor. Restored in 1949 and again refurbished in the last few years, the house retains its fine timbered walls, the upper storey built outwards on wooden corbels to gain more space. A queen's head is actually carved onto one of the beam-ends.

12. Quays and Locks
PARK SQUARE, S2

The recently refurbished and re-named Victoria Quays has been one of the great successes in Sheffield's belated attempt to preserve something of its glorious commercial past – despite attempts only recently to fill it in and build a car park! The idea for a Sheffield canal was first suggested in 1697 but it wasn't until the Napoleonic Wars (1815) that the demand for Sheffield-made swords and cannon balls forced its construction. The 20 million gallon canal basin welcomed its first boats on 22nd February 1819 and it was reported that "the oldest man in Sheffield never saw such a day". Coal, iron, timber, grain and turnips flooded in on "Sheffield-size" keels, designed specially to accommodate the locks. However, by 1840 the railways brought decline and a last cargo of maize was delivered in December 1970. Amongst the many interesting buildings are the Merchants' Crescent which housed coal offices; Sheaf Works (now a pub) which was the first entirely steam-driven works; the Grain Warehouse from where grain was dispatched to mills and breweries; and the 'Straddle', a grain warehouse ingeniously built over the canal when building space became limited.

13. Underneath the Arches
THE WICKER, S4

At the bottom of Spital Hill, near the Wicker Arches, is a huge brick gatepost beyond which was Sheffield's first railway station built in 1838 at the terminus of the Sheffield and Rotherham Railway. Its completion enabled the expansion of large scale steelworks in the Lower Don Valley. In 1870 it became a goods yard when the direct line through Midland Station opened, and in 1962 it was closed. The wall supporting Spital Hill still has a ramp up which horses were led to railway stables next to the Arches. It also contains a blocked tunnel of 1849 which led to Bridgehouses Station where it joined the Sheffield, Ashton-under-Lyne and Manchester Railway. The Arches themselves were built in 1849 as part of a 40-arch viaduct carrying the new Manchester, Sheffield and Lincolnshire Railway over the Don Valley. It was built by Sheffield engineer William Fowler, who built the Forth Railway Bridge. At the east side was a lift taking passengers to the former Victoria Station (1851-1970) where a single forlorn gantry remains from Britain's first electrified line. The station is gone but the railway hotel remains, which once boasted England's finest cooked breakfast! Inside the arches is a memorial listing 1,304 Great Central Railwaymen who died in the Great War.

14. When the Zeppelins Came
EFFINGHAM ROAD, S4

There is a sad reminder of the human toll inflicted by the First World War on Effingham Road at the Baltic Works, itself an original crucible steel shop set up by Joseph Beardshaw & Son in 1854. On the outside wall of the fine office block is a stone memorial marking the site where, on the 26th September 1916, 9 men, 10 women and 10 children perished during an air raid. 36 bombs were dropped by a German Zeppelin, one of the occasional airship raids made on the Midlands and the North of England. The main targets were London and the Southeast.

During World War Two, a German bombing raid on the steel and munitions factories of the East End destroyed a fine castle-like lockhouse on the Sheffield and Tinsley canal nearby. Despite damage to the area, production continued throughout the war.

15. Guns and Hammers
SAVILE STREET EAST, S4

Twenty years ago Sheffield's Lower Don Valley still showed signs of what was once Europe's most concentrated area of heavy engineering. All the great names were here, the dazzle of molten steel shining below doorways and the sound of hammers filling the air. Although still a centre for special steels much of the heavy industry has gone leaving huge spaces for redevelopment. Thankfully some reminders are left. On Savile Street East is a 5-ton steam hammer (pictured) built by Brightside Foundry and Engineering Ltd. in 1947 for Brown Bayley and later moved to Firth Brown to forge steel railway wheels and bearings. It is now a monument on the former site of Cammell's East Forge. Such hammers, invented in 1839 in Manchester, superseded water-powered tilt hammers (see no. 34). On Carlisle Street behind is Bessemer's 1905 office block, of Bessemer converter fame (see no. 48). Also on Savile Street East is the re-built gateway of Thomas Firth's 'Siemen's Dept.', an open hearth process which produced more steel than a converter. Preserved nearby is the West Gun Works built by Firths in the 1860's where the famous Enfield rifle was produced.

16. Huntsman's Old Home
WORKSOP ROAD, S9

A plaque on the wall of the Britannia Inn on Worksop Road states that the building was believed to have been the home of Benjamin Huntsman (1704-1776), the inventor of crucible steel (see no. 34) and founder of Sheffield's reputation for quality steel. The date '1772' on the gable end of the building is rumoured to be made of crucible steel and records the setting up of his nearby Attercliffe Works. Huntsman is buried at the Hilltop Chapel nearby (see no. 18). Another pub, the King's Head on Attercliffe Common, was once the village chemist where Samuel Jackson, co-founder of Spear and Jackson, was born in 1839. As a pub it was home to George Littlewood (1859-1912), world champion endurance racer.

Another Attercliffe hostelry, the Carbrook Hall Hotel, is cited as the city's most haunted public house. It was built c. 1623 by the Bright family from which Colonel John Bright of Cromwell's army rode to York for help when Sheffield Castle was threatened by Royalist troops.

17. Attercliffe's Legacy of Leisure
LEEDS ROAD, S9

Tucked away on Leeds Road by the side of the recently built, high-tech Stadium is a large and fine red-brick building which once catered for the leisure needs of the inhabitants of Victorian Attercliffe. At one end is Attercliffe Library which opened in 1894 in answer to local public demand and didn't close its doors until 1986. As well as lending books it was one of the first places in Sheffield to display lists of job vacancies.

At the other end is Attercliffe Baths built in 1879 to provide both swimming and washing facilities for the area at a time when bathrooms at home were almost unknown. This was also Attercliffe's 'speakers corner', especially between 1900 and 1939.

Opposite, on Vicarage Road, is the old Adelphi Picture Theatre, its exotic colourful facade now restored for its new use as a nightclub. Opened in 1920 it showed films until 1967 serving also, like so many of Sheffield's cinemas, as a bingo hall.

18. The Hill Top Chapel
ATTERCLIFFE COMMON, S9

Almost hidden by trees in the corner of a leafy graveyard on Attercliffe Common can be found the Hill Top Chapel. Built in 1629 it opened for worship on October 10th 1630, the bulk of its construction cost (£102) being borne by the Bright family of nearby Carbrook Hall (see no. 16). It is the oldest place of worship in the valley and remained the sole Anglican church for Attercliffe until 1826. It has subsequently been remodelled. The surrounding churchyard contains memorials to several famous Attercliffe citizens, including Benjamin Huntsman, the inventor of crucible steel (see no. 16). To this day the churchyard retains an air of old-world tranquility.

Also of religious interest is the Attercliffe Vestry Hall on Attercliffe Common. Built in the 1860's it became Sheffield's first family planning clinic in the 1930's. Adjacent is a fine red-brick house where Sir R.A. Hadfield was born who went on to become world famous in the development of alloy steels.

19. Sheffield's Own Dick Turpin
BROUGHTON LANE, S9

On Broughton Lane, opposite the 10,000 seat Sheffield Arena built in 1991, is the intriguingly named 'Noose and Gibbet' public house. The replica gibbet outside *(see front cover)* contains an effigy of highwayman Spence Broughton, after whom the road was named. Broughton was a gentleman farmer from Lincoln who married well and received a handsome dowry but squandered it through gambling at cock fights. To recoup his loss he turned to crime becoming a member of the Hatters Club, a local band of Attercliffe villains. However, his life of crime was short-lived being hung in the 1790's for the robbery of the Sheffield mail on Attercliffe Common. He was hung and gibbeted in chains close to the site of the pub where his remains were left on view for 27 years as a deterrent to would-be thieves and brigands. He was the last man to be so treated in England. The pub, as well as serving a good pint, contains numerous depictions of Broughton and the Hatters Club and includes the highwayman's hand – allegedly!

20. At the End of the Tram Line
WEEDON STREET, S9

Sheffield once boasted the first, last and one of the most extensive tram networks of any English city (see no. 5). Although now partially replaced by the Supertram, the heyday of the classic tram is now long gone. The only tangible reminder of the original system are the few remaining depots where trams would be repaired and stored overnight. On Leadmill Road is the Shoreham Street Tram Depot built in 1920 with ornate turrets framing its lofty entrance. The Heeley horse-drawn tram depot still exists at the bottom of Albert Road, and another, at the top of Sheldon Road now contains a supermarket. The most interesting is the Tinsley Tram Depot on Weedon Street, built in 1874 for horse trams and extended in 1899 for electric trams. The inscription "SHEFFIELD TRAMWAYS COMPANY' can still be seen on the oldest part of the building (pictured). Sheffield's last tram terminated here in 1960. At present it houses the Sheffield Bus Museum which contains a fascinating collection of bus and tram memorabilia. It is funded and managed solely by dedicated enthusiasts.

21. A Grand Canyon in the East End
BRIGHTSIDE LANE, S9

Surely one of the most visual reminders of Sheffield's industrial heyday (see no. 15) must be the imposing Vickers Building on Brightside Lane. Together with the River Don Works opposite, it forms the last example of 'canyon' architecture, the two facades giving the effect of a street of New York skyscrapers. The Vickers building was erected in 1907 as head office for the steel and munitions giant. It was designed by the architects Holmes and Watson (!) and was luxuriously finished in marble. The building to the left was added in 1910 and has cast iron lintels proudly marked 'V' (Vickers) and 'VSM' (Vickers Son & Maxim). It was later occupied by English Steel, British Steel and Sheffield Forgemasters but is now awaiting re-use. The mighty River Don Works opposite were founded in 1863 by Naylor Vickers and has long specialised in the heaviest forgings and castings for the shipbuilding, energy and defence industries which Sheffield Forgemasters still continue. It once held the world's largest crucible steelworks and the now demolished North Gun Shop (1902) was the world's first engineering workshop to be entirely electric powered.

22. The Cholera Monument
NORFOLK ROAD, S2

The Memorial Gardens on Norfolk Road are so-named because they contain Sheffield's Cholera Monument. The obelisk marks the mass burial site of 402 people who died during an epidemic of Asiatic cholera in 1832. Some 1,347 people were afflicted in total. The disease had appeared in England in 1831 and gradually spread across the country, assisted by poor sanitary conditions and open drains. The foundation stone was laid by the poet James Montgomery on December 11th 1834 and the topstone, which toppled in the 1990 hurricane, was added on April 11th 1835. Nearby is the grave of John Blake, Master Cutler, who succumbed to cholera on August 30th 1832 aged 49 years and in his 12th month of office. His gravestone records how he perished after only a few hours illness and was buried the same day "in this secluded spot" along with his fellow townsfolk who died of the same "calamitous infliction". The stone was erected by his surviving brothers.

Opposite the gardens are the Shrewsbury Alms Houses built in 1827 for the elderly and infirm and founded originally by the 17th Earl of Shrewsbury as a charity in 1617.

23. Where Mary Queen of Scots Stayed
MANOR ROAD, S2

The remains of Sheffield's Manor house stand high above the city in what was once the deer park of the Earls of Shrewsbury, Lords of the Manor. In those days the little town of Sheffield lay two or so miles away. The once magnificent house, built c. 1510 by the 4th Earl, is now in ruins having been dismantled in 1706 and left derelict ever since. Amongst the remaining shattered walls is Wolsey's Tower, the disgraced archbishop having visited the manor after his fall in 1529. The only part to remain intact is an Elizabethan summer house, known as the Turret House, dating to 1574. Mary Queen of Scots, Sheffield's most celebrated prisoner, was held captive here and at Sheffield Castle (see no. 9) by the 6th Earl between 1570 and 1584. Today, the Turret House contains an exhibition describing both the Manor and Mary's imprisonment, its finely plastered upper room said to be where the Queen was periodically confined.

24. Europe's Oldest Glass Kiln
CHURCH LANE, S60

The conical, brick-built kiln which pierces the horizon at Catcliffe is a rare survival of the glass industry which flourished in South Yorkshire from the early eighteenth century. Barnsley was its centre where Hiram Codd invented his famous bottle with an integrated marble stopper to retain the 'fizz' in carbonated drinks. Catcliffe cone was built in c.1740 by William Fenny who had come here from the glass works at Bolsterstone. Some 68 feet high and 40 feet wide it is one of only half a dozen left in Britain and is the oldest of its type in Europe. Now empty, its arches around the base once led to a series of furnaces where the glass was 'founded'. The arches were sealed to produce a draught through the furnace whereas the surrounding cone itself restricted air circulation to prevent loss of heat when the glass was removed as well as to extract poisonous fumes. Once one of a pair, such structures were the standard, all-in-one, glass-making buildings for a century or so. Although Catcliffe cone closed in the 1880's it did re-open, unsuccessfully, for a year in 1901. It has recently been renovated and is open to view.

25. Taking the Waters
BIRLEY SPA LANE, S12

At the bottom of Birley Spa Lane, in a small wooded valley, can be found South Yorkshire's most impressive and intact commercial spa building. That a good water supply had been long recognised in the vicinity is proven by the discovery of Stone Age tools and a Roman road nearby. The present building dates to the 1840's and still contains a huge bath 25 by 18 feet in size with a depth of 6 feet. An eighteenth century guide describes the Birley water as 'chalybeate' (i.e. containing iron) and abounding "with volatile vitriol"! No wonder people flocked to take the waters in order to relieve all manner of complaints, such as wounds and swellings. An 1843 analysis showed sulphate of soda, which prevented constipation caused when using chalybeate cures, and carbonic acid, which increased the tonic power of the water and made it agree better with the stomach. After the outbreak of war in 1939 the spa closed and became increasingly dilapidated. Although nearly demolished in 1960 it is now a listed building which, together with its lovely grounds, has been restored.

26. Stars of Stage and Screen
LONDON ROAD, S8

A glance at the 'Sheffield Star' from 40 to 50 years ago would remind the reader that Sheffield once boasted 53 cinemas. The 'picture palaces' gradually succumbed to television and, although some served as bingo halls and supermarkets, many were demolished. At the start of London Road there still exists the former Lansdowne Picture Palace (pictured) which opened in 1914 with 1500 seats. It closed in 1940 following Blitz damage and a purchase offer from Marks and Spencer. Since 1954 it has been a series of dance halls and clubs. Further along is the equally exotic-looking Abbeydale Picture House (1920-1975), the only cinema to be listed for protection. A snooker hall now occupies its basement ballroom. Nearby at number 377 Abbeydale Road is a former Temperance Bar where teetotallers once took refreshments. Finally, on Kenwood Park Road is the tiny Lantern Theatre (formerly the Chalet Theatre) built in 1898 by a wealthy cutler for private performances and now fully renovated and re-opened.

27. Two Unknown Sheffielders

STAVELEY ROAD, S8

Within a stone's throw of each other, at 20-22 Staveley Road and 99-101 Abbeydale Road, are two carved male heads whose identity is today a mystery.

The former once adorned a row of older houses which were demolished in 1978, the head being incorporated into the modern houses that replaced them. The aristocratic, bearded man in question was nicknamed 'Lord Staveley' and for many years it was the custom for men passing by to lift their hats in respect. Unfortunately, local records do not list a Lord Staveley. Even more curious is the fact that a very similar head has just been spotted not far away at the junction of Countess Road and John Street.

Even less is known about the second head on Abbeydale Road which was built into a row of Victorian houses. It seems to be a man wearing a helmet – possibly a lost soldier? Who knows . . . ?

28. The Mansion That Became a Laundry
BARMOUTH ROAD, S7

Hidden behind an unattractive modern warehouse at the junction of Abbeydale and Woodseats Road is the once grand Abbeydale House. It was built in 1849 for John Rodgers, whose father founded one of Sheffield's most famous cutlery firms, Joseph Rodgers and Sons. The house was constructed of polished Anston stone in the Italian style and Rodgers lived here until his death 10 years later. The business then passed to his nephew Robert Newbould who built Abbeydale Grange further up the road. The mansion was then auctioned, the brochure listing its dining room, drawing room, library, boudoir, servants' hall, butler's pantry, housekeeper's room and six bedrooms. Between 1903 and 1906 it was the office of the Snowite Laundry who had their boardroom on the first floor. Their fleet of Morris Oxford delivery vans was once a common sight on Barmouth Road. Sadly, the house is today an empty shell, its glory days a distant memory.

29. Sheffield's Brontë Connection
GLEADLESS ROAD, S8

Christ's Church on Gleadless Road, Heeley is a fine historic building in itself but, like most older churches, it also boasts several associated curiosities.

The gateway into the churchyard was erected to the memory of Thomas Axelby Earnshaw, Lance Corporal in the Royal Welsh Fusiliers, who was killed in France on April 25th 1916. The gate was financed by the soldier's parents in September 1919 and a plaque carries Psalm 100-104: "Enter into His gates with thanksgiving".

Once inside the churchyard, immediately on the left, can be seen a large obelisk to the memory of John Shortridge of Chipping House, Abbeydale, who was responsible for the construction of the Sheffield-Manchester Railway and the Wicker Arches. The huge granite base which supports the obelisk required 20 horses to tow it to the churchyard.

Finally, inside the church itself, near the chancel, is a memorial to surgeon Thomas Wooler of Dewsbury who died in 1895 aged 92. He retired to Heeley and was brother of Margaret Wooler, friend and school mistress of Charlotte Brontë.

30. Bishops, Ruskin and the Oddfellows
NORTON LEES LANE, S8

At the southeast entrance to Meersbrook Park in Norton Lees Lane is the so-called Bishop's House, a delightful, if much restored, timber-framed farmhouse built c. 1500. It retains many original features and is the best preserved and earliest example of a timbered house to have survived in Sheffield. The northwest end, which is stone, is a seventeenth century extension built by Captain William Blythe, a prosperous farmer, miller, scythe manufacturer and Parliamentarian, after the Civil War. Today the building is a museum containing rooms furnished in period style. There is no definite proof that a bishop ever lived here and the name is of recent origin.

At the Brook Road entrance to the Park is the former house of Benjamin Roebuck which became the famous Ruskin Museum. Now council offices, this red-brick building once housed Ruskin's collection of art and artefacts to which devotees from around the globe came to pay homage. Some of his collection now resides in the Ruskin Gallery on Norfolk Street.

One final curiosity in Meersbrook Park is a small and ornate drinking fountain, also close to Brook Road, which is dedicated to the memory of a former secretary of the Oddfellows Association.

31. From Donkey Boy to Sculptor
NORTON LANE, S8

Sir Francis Chantrey (1781-1841), one of England's greatest ever sculptors, was born to a carpenter at Norton, then a village 4 miles from Sheffield. Such were his later achievements that the area became known as "Chantreyland". His early years were spent working for a grocer, occasionally delivering barrels of milk to Sheffield on a donkey. Between 1797 and 1802 he was apprenticed to a carver and gilder, finishing early to take up as a portrait painter in Paradise Square. He also studied sculpture at the Royal Academy in London discovering that this was his true skill. After his first work in 1806, a bust of the vicar of Sheffield, he moved to London and never looked back. He became a member of the R.A. in 1818 and was knighted by William IV in 1835. He produced statues for Worcester and Lichfield cathedrals, busts of Wellington, Wordsworth and Scott, and sculpted no less than four English sovereigns from life. Chantrey left instructions to be interred in his beloved Norton churchyard, close to which is an obelisk (pictured) erected in 1854 to his memory by his friend Philip Hardwick, R.A.

32. The Well That Never Runs Dry
GRAVES PARK, S8

Alongside a footpath by the stream which flows through Waterfall Wood from the boating lake in Graves Park, is a curious well. Henry Tatton, in his book *"Sheffield"* (1926), called it "the Mystery Well of Graves Park . . . (of which) nothing is known of its history, except a 'wishing well'. It never freezes, runs dry or alters in depth. At one time, Norton's only water supply". It is surrounded by a stone canopy and remains a true oddity to this day.

There are numerous literary references to other Sheffield wells, such as Pond Street Spa, but whose locations are long since lost. However, Monk's Well still exists down some stone steps in quiet woodland adjacent to Beauchief Abbey Lane. It was described in the*"Sheffield Star"* (1935) as "one of the most famous drinking springs in this country for the cure of alcoholic illnesses" with "perhaps the coldest water in all England . . . a real tonic"!

33. Memories of Thomas à Beckett
ABBEY LANE, S8

The romantic ruins of Beauchief Abbey date back to the late twelfth century when it was occupied by an offshoot of the Augustinian order of monks. Legend states it was founded by Robert Fitz-Ranulph, remorseful for his part in the murder of Thomas à Beckett in Canterbury Cathedral. Such was his guilt he not only built and endowed the abbey but dedicated it to the archbishop. Today only the picturesque west tower remains, its great window now robbed of its original flowing tracery. Behind is a chapel-like nave added c.1660 and on the left is an original Norman doorway. On the right is a later doorway from the fourteenth century, both of which have been re-built from remains found in the surrounding gardens. The chapel still has its seventeenth century furnishings including box pews, reading desk, pulpit and family pews for the squire and rector. Further up the lane, past the Monk's well (see no. 32) is the stately Beauchief Hall built in 1671.

34. Crucible Steel and Charcoal Burning

ABBEYDALE ROAD SOUTH, S8

Abbeydale Industrial Hamlet is a unique preserved example of a water-powered works from before the days of steam. During the eighteenth and nineteenth centuries a wheel, 18 feet in diameter powered by the Sheaf, drove two tilt hammers which shaped scythe blades made of 'blister steel' (see no. 51) welded between two layers of iron. The steel was melted at 1550°C in clay pots known as 'crucibles', a technique pioneered by Benjamin Huntsman (see no. 16) which, for the first time, allowed steel to be cast as an ingot. Once welded to the iron, the bar was heated and forged under a steeling hammer then cut to size, reheated and shaped into a blade under the plating hammer. The roughly forged blades were then tempered in a hand forge, sharpened in the grinding shop on millstone grit wheels and attached to a spine. The charcoal used in the crucible furnace may well have come from charcoal burner George Yardley who burned to death and is buried in Ecclesall Woods nearby (see page 64).

35. England's First King
VICARAGE LANE, S17

On the village green at Dore can be found a small sandstone monolith bearing a plaque in the shape of a Saxon shield. It relates how on this spot in A.D. 829 King Ecgbert of Wessex accepted the submission of King Eanred of Northumberland, thus becoming the first overlord of all England. Prior to this the land was divided into the three warring Saxon Kingdoms of Wessex (south west), Mercia (south east) and Northumberland (north), each eager to gain supremacy. It fell to Ecgbert, meaning 'Bright Sword', to subjugate Mercia and march north to the border which lay at Dore. Far from the bloody fight expected, the Anglo Saxon Chronicle relates how Eanred came peacefully, probably because Northumberland faced a greater threat from marauding Scandinavians on the North Sea. Ecgbert's grandson, Alfred the Great, continued the unification process. Also in Dore can be seen the ancient Derbyshire custom of well dressing, reflecting the fact that the village once lay in that county.

36. Lost Art in a Supermarket
ECCLESALL ROAD, S11

The Safeway supermarket at the bottom of Ecclesall Road looks like any other modern store across the country. However, it is different in that its foyer contains a piece of architectural history. Until a few years ago the site was occupied by the Co-op, a much loved department store with a white stone exterior, broken at intervals by colourful depictions of flowers in vases. These were rendered in glazed tiles, or faience, known as "Carrara Ware" manufactured in 1929 by Messrs. Doulton of Lambeth, London. The secrets of the manufacturing process are now lost but fortunately one of the decorations has been saved and can be seen in the new supermarket.

Next door, at the junction with London Road, is an old bank building now occupied by a shop. At pavement level can be seen an old milestone giving directions to Hathersage, Castleton and Chapel-en-le-Frith. This once important road is now a cul-de-sac.

37. The Home of Sheffield Bitter

ECCLESALL ROAD, S11

Brewing was once a large industry in South Yorkshire but in Sheffield only Ward's Sheaf Brewery on Ecclesall Road, Stones Cannon Brewery on Rutland Road and a few recent real-ale breweries are still in production.

The Soho Brewery of Bradley and Co. had set up at Ecclesall Road in 1837. Wards began shortly afterwards in 1840 and came here in the early 1870's bringing the 'Sheaf' name with them. The site is dominated by a five-storey 'brewing tower' built in 1874 which is still in use. Brewing towers were developed in the 1860's to enable each of the successive stages of beer production to take place on different levels. Water was pumped to the top by steam power and the liquor, mixed with malted barley and hops, passed down through the various stages by gravity. The accompanying smell on the streets below can be quite overwhelming! The gateway (pictured) to the brewery, like those of the recently closed Whitbread's Exchange Brewery on Lady's Bridge, is adorned with sheaves of corn. It was moved and re-built in the early 1980's.

38. Art is Long, Life is Short

GLOSSOP ROAD, S10

Incorporated into a modern brick wall on the southwest side of the Royal Hallamshire Hospital on Glossop Road is the curious inscription "ARS LONGA VITA BREVIS". Translated into English it reads "Art is long, life is short", which may seem odd reading for those entering the hospital. However, the inscription was originally incorporated into the facade of the now demolished Medical School on Surrey Street, now occupied by the City Library and Graves Art Gallery. The building housed the school from 1828, when it was built, until 1888 after which it served as an army recruiting centre. The Latin motto is ascribed to the Greek scholar Hippocrates (400 B.C.) and refers to the difficulty in acquiring and practising the art of medicine. The same motto is also carved over the door of another old medical school in Leopold Street.

The garden in front of the Hallamshire Hospital contains a small monument to Robert Ernest, M.D., first house surgeon of the old General Infirmary. During his 44 years of service 88,000 patients passed under his care and 48,000 children were vaccinated.

39. Grave Situations !

CEMETERY ROAD, S11

All great English cities possess at least one rambling Victorian cemetery crammed with monuments, family vaults, temples and Gothic fancies, and Sheffield is no exception. In 1836 a private company opened the General Cemetery between Ecclesall Road and Cemetery Road in response to a demand for quality burial places for non-conformists, that is people not belonging to the Church of England. It was one of the first public cemeteries in the country and eased pressure on the City Centre churchyards following the cholera epidemic of the 1830's (see no. 22). Occupying the western part of today's cemetery, it is dominated by the Egyptian Chapel (pictured) and is entered by the Lion Gate which crosses the Porter Brook near Ecclesall Road. In 1850, the cemetery was extended eastwards to Montague Street, beyond what is known as the Dissenters' Wall. Dominated by the spired Church of England Chapel, this is where Anglican burials were made. A statue of the poet James Montgomery once stood in front of the Chapel. Although the 1970's saw widespread clearance and dilapidation, the General Cemetery is still a fascinating place containing the graves of Sheffield Chartist Samuel Holberry and steel magnate Mark Firth.

40. A Pinch of Sheffield Snuff
SHARROW VALE ROAD, S11

Off Sharrow Vale Road, almost hidden from view by trees, is a hidden corner of old Sheffield. Across a mirror-smooth dam can be glimpsed Wilson's snuff mill, built in 1763. A grinding wheel existed here as early as 1604 which was leased, in 1738, to Thomas Wilson, shearsmith. However, it was down to Joseph Wilson to introduce snuff grinding in the 1740's. Although steam power was introduced in 1796 and the works have used electricity since 1956, the original water-powered snuff mill, using culverted water from the River Porter, is still in use. Wilson's snuff is still flavoured in secret behind closed doors, only one person per generation being made privy to the unique combination of ingredients. Viewing is by appointment only but the effort is well worth it for the overpowering smell alone!

41. If You Go Down to the Woods Today
CLARKEHOUSE ROAD, S11

Sheffield's Botanical Gardens, with entrances on Clarkehouse Road and Ecclesall Road, were opened in 1836. In those days, these 20 beautiful acres were available only to the wealthy, access being possible by a ten shilling and 6d. token. Private access ceased in 1898 since when the gardens have been owned by the Town Trustees. In 1951 they were leased to the council for a shilling.

There are numerous curiosities here including Joseph Paxton's trio of miniature crystal palaces built of glass and cast iron. On a nearby hillock is a bearpit where parading Victorians could get a taste of the wild. Also to be found is a fossilised tree stump discovered during coal mining on the site of the Midland Railway Station. It is some 300 million years old. Finally, there is the Crimean War Memorial which once stood atop a column at Moorhead in the city centre. When the statue of Victory was moved to the gardens in 1960 the column was re-used in a children's playground in Hammond Street (see no. 52).

42. Queen Victoria and an American Bomber
ENDCLIFFE PARK, S11

Endcliffe Park can boast no less than two monuments associated with Queen Victoria, both of which were originally erected elsewhere.

The Queen's Monolith with its broad platform and four standard lamps commemorated Victoria's Jubilee in 1887 and stood originally in the Town Hall Square where it became a popular meeting place. When it was moved to the far end of Endcliffe Park it was replaced by a statue of Queen Victoria. The stone pedestal on which it stands bears sculptures of a man with a hammer ('Labour') and a woman and child ('Maternity'). This too was moved to the Park close to the Hunters Bar entrance. The site is today occupied by the Goodwin Fountain, a gift to the City by two of its most famous benefactors, Sir Stuart and Lady Goodwin.

Also in Endcliffe Park, beyond the famous stepping stones across the River Porter, is a monument to the 10-man crew of an American Flying Fortress bomber, the 'Mi Amigo', which was damaged over Germany in 1944 and crashed on this spot (pictured). All the men perished in their effort to avoid the houses below.

43. The Salt Box

PSALTER LANE, S11

At the brow of Psalter Lane, where it drops down towards Banner Cross with its memories of Sheffield criminal Charlie Peace, can be found an outcrop of natural rock with a few square holes cut into its surface. Today, it is hard to imagine that these holes once held timber joists which supported the upper floors of the Saltbox Cottages, a well known landmark for many years. Their unusual name is thought by some to be because the building had the appearance of an old saltbox hanging on a kitchen wall. This would have been accentuated when the road was lowered in the mid-1800's to reduce the steep gradient at this point. Alternatively, the name is linked with Psalter Lane, the road being part of the original and ancient route taken by packhorse trains bringing shipments of salt into the City from distant Cheshire via Manchester. The cottages, built in the late eighteenth century and largely dismantled by 1969, were once home to the proprietor of Brincliffe Quarry, outcrops of which still exist.

44. Wayside Curiosities
CARTERKNOWLE ROAD, S11

Towards the top of Carterknowle Road is a seemingly ordinary red cast-iron pillar box which the authors passed on numerous occasions before noticing the unusual cipher embossed on it – that of Edward VIII. The shortness of his reign (January – December 1936), due to his abdication to marry Wallis Simpson, ensured that such boxes are very rare. Other examples of old pillar boxes in Sheffield include Victorian ones on Fulwood Road, Brincliffe Edge Road and the Cathedral forecourt, and one from the reign of Edward VII at Woodhouse.

Another pavement oddity still to be found are the large grey and green cylinders of the type found on Highcliffe Road and Barnsley Road. Inscribed "The British Electric Transformer Co., Hayes, Middlesex" they were used in the early distribution of power to the suburbs of Sheffield.

45. Mr. Shepherd's Grinding Shop
HANGINGWATER ROAD, S11

Beside the River Porter in Whiteley Woods is a man-made dam which once turned the Shepherd Wheel. It is one of the few remaining examples of the water-powered grinding works (or 'hulls') once common along the rivers of nineteenth century Sheffield. It contains two workshops each containing grindstones used to sharpen knives and to put points on forks. Shepherd Wheel is possibly the "Potar Whele" recorded in a will of 1584 and is named after a Mr. Shepherd who employed 10 men here in 1794. Although last worked in the 1930's, the works and waterwheel remain intact as a museum. Along one side of the building there is an unusual staircase built of discarded grindstones (pictured). A Sheffield doctor produced statistics in the 1840's which showed that 50% of fork-grinders died before 30 because of the metal and stone dust which attacked the lungs.

46. The Inventor of Sheffield Plate
WHITELEY WOOD ROAD, S11

Hidden in woods alongside Wiremill Dam is a monument inscribed as follows: "This memorial was erected partly of the stones from a mill built near this place by Thomas Boulsover, the inventor of Sheffield Plate born 1705 died 1788. He carried on his industries here and resided at Whiteley Wood Hall from 1762 until his death. Erected by David Flather Master Cutler 1926-27". In 1742 Boulsover, a Quaker clockmaker from Doncaster, invented the technique of producing silver plated articles by rolling ingots of silver-coated copper into sheets. This was the origin of the important industry of manufacturing Old Sheffield Plate. This was superseded 100 years later by electro-plating. His original works were in the city centre on Norfolk Street where the Crucible Theatre stage door now stands.

Further up Whiteley Wood Road, at the junction with Trap Lane, is a Methodist Chapel built in 1789 to Boulsover's memory by his daughters Mary Mitchell and Sarah Hutton.

47. Toll Gates and Milestones
RINGINGLOW ROAD, S11

As an ever-developing city, Sheffield's myriad roads have been re-surfaced and widened so often that little of the original routes remain. During the eighteenth and nineteenth centuries many roads were turnpiked, that is properly surfaced and paid for by the collection of tolls from travellers. At Ringinglow there still remains the quaint octagonal Barber Fields tollhouse (pictured) built c.1795. It stands on the 1758 Sheffield turnpike where it divided to Fox House / Buxton and Hathersage / Chapel-en-le-Frith. Known as the Round House its gates are gone, but it is still accompanied by the Norfolk Arms where turnpike travellers sought refreshment. A milestone can be seen against the car park wall. A restored tollgate or bar exists on Hunters Bar roundabout which once had a horse trough now languishing in a field off Hangram Lane. Other tollhouses exist at the bottom of Collegiate Crescent and at the junction of Burngreave and Pitsmoor Roads, on the Sheffield-Leeds turnpike of 1758.

48. Steel By the Bucket Load!
ALMA STREET, S3

A milestone in the nineteenth century steel revolution was the invention of the Converter in 1855 by Henry Bessemer (1813-98) whereby bulk steel could be made quickly and cheaply by blowing air through molten iron in a huge pear-shaped vessel. He set up the first commercial Bessemer melting shop in Sheffield in 1858 giving licences to John Brown, Cammell and Samuel Fox leading to the world-wide introduction of cheap bulk steel. Later Siemen's open hearth furnace produced higher quality steel and both processes made Sheffield the leading centre for the armaments industry. Local companies could now make steel, roll it, forge it under hammers and churn out armour, ship and boiler plates and guns all on the same site. Although both processes are now extinct in Britain, the last Bessemer converter used, at Workington in 1974, is preserved together with the 12000 h.p. River Don steam engine (1905) at Kelham Island Industrial Museum on Alma Street. The bulk steel trade eventually moved to the ore fields and the coast where iron and steel could be made on one site leaving Sheffield to concentrate on engineering and alloy steel.

49. A Saw Point!

BALL STREET, S3

Approaching Penistone Road by the Ball Street bridge, which crosses the River Don, itself lined with old factories and weirs, a fine piece of period advertising can be seen. Covering a gable end is a plaster sign reading "ALFRED BECKETT & SONS LTD. STEEL, SAW & FILE WORKS, CORPORATE MARK MATCHLESS". Alfred Beckett established a saw-making business in 1839 and came here, from original premises in Beet Street, in 1865. He brought with him the name 'Brooklyn Works' reflecting his trade with North America. A 1948 letter head advertised cast steel, combined iron and steel, high speed steel, rustless and stainless steel, files, circular and band saws, circular cold saws, shear blades and machine knives, all manufactured under his 'Matchless' trademark.

Over the road is the once mighty Cornish Place, founded by James Dixon in 1822 to make cutlery, plated goods and the silver-like 'Britannia Metal'. The site covers 4 acres and once employed 800 people but today lies empty.

50. When Sheffield Ruled the World
PENISTONE LANE, S6

Whilst much of Sheffield's heavy industry was focused in the East End (see nos. 15 & 21), it should not be forgotten that earlier foundries and edge-tool works were nearer to, and indeed in, the city centre. 'Little Mesters' workshops can still be seen on Garden Street and behind the Howard Hotel on Surrey Lane. However, it is around Kelham Island (see no. 48) that entire streets of works still exist, albeit empty or converted, from which products were exported worldwide. On Penistone Lane is the fine classical facade of the Globe Works, at one end of which are the owner's house and offices (pictured). It was built in 1825 for Ibbotson and Roebuck, makers of refined steel, scythes, saws and knives. The works were attacked in 1843 for bad working conditions. Between 1825 and 1973 some 74 firms were here, the last being hand-cutters of files and rasps in 1980. Nearby is Henry Hoole's Green Lane Works founded in 1795 for the production of stove grates, a speciality of South Yorkshire iron works. Hoole was Mayor in 1860 and celebrated this with the erection of a triumphal arch. Today it is occupied by the engineering firm W.A. Tyzack.

51. The Origin of 'Crozzle' !

HOYLE STREET, S3

There are numerous old stone walls along the roads of the East End, and other former industrial areas, which are topped with a black, lava-like material known locally as 'crozzle'. This almost indestructible substance was a by-product of a steel manufacturing process known as the 'Cementation Process'. On Hoyle Street behind Sheffield University is the last intact example of Sheffield's 260 cementation furnaces. It was part of the Daniel Doncaster works built in the 1830's and last fired in 1951. It contains two stone chests in which iron bars and charcoal were heated for up to 3 weeks. This produced 35 tons of 'blister steel', so-called because of the bubbles it contained, which would then be refined in crucible furnaces (see no. 34). The crust removed from the top of the chests when the steel was ready became 'crozzle'. An unusual anti-glare device can be seen on top of the furnace to prevent night time detection by enemy bombers during the Second World War.

52. A Playground with a Difference
HAMMOND STREET, S3

Surrounded by modern housing on Hammond Street in Netherthorpe is a playground. The centrepiece is a group of stone drums whose finely cut surfaces suggests they once had a grander use. Indeed, they once formed a mighty column which supported a statue of Victoria as "Honour" at Moorhead. Known as the Crimean War Memorial it was erected in 1857 by the public subscription of £1,400, one subscriber being Florence Nightingale. The well known landmark commemorated the fallen soldiers and sailors of that grim Russian war (1854-56) and appears on many old photographs of Moorhead. However, it was dismantled in 1960 during which a plate recording the architect was discovered. The statue and its base found a new home in the Botanical Gardens (see no. 41) but the 18 feet high column of Aberdeen granite was cut up and placed on Hammond Street where it can still be found.

53. The Corn Law Rhymer
BLAKEGROVE ROAD, S6

The grand house which still stands at the end of Blakegrove Road was once home to Ebenezer Elliott (1781-1849). Born in Rotherham, he inherited an iron foundry but after becoming bankrupt at the age of 40, he moved his wife and nine children to Sheffield – in a cart! He had an obsessive dislike of the Corn Laws seeing them as a tax on bread causing the poverty of his fellow men whilst favouring the farmers. He aired his views in a series of political writings including the famous "Corn Law Rhymes" in 1831. To his delight the laws were repealed in 1846 following the failure of both Irish potato and English corn crops. Elliott also wrote gentler poems extolling the rural delights of Hallamshire such as "Farewell to Rivelin". He eventually became a prosperous iron and steel merchant enabling him to live in his fine house. A statue of Elliott adorns Weston Park to this day.

54. Waterloo and the Light Brigade
LANGSETT ROAD, S6

The classic *"Illustrated Guide to Sheffield and Neighbourhood"* published in 1862 by local publishers Pawson and Brailsford, described the Sheffield Barracks as being "amongst the very finest in the Kingdom . . . . quite in the outskirts of the town, on a salubrious spot, and commanding magnificent views of the surrounding scenery." Today the castellated building lies in the heart of Hillsborough and contains businesses and a large supermarket. When built in 1850 it was known as the New Barracks, having replaced an older building also on Langsett Road but nearer to the town centre. A notable feature of the New Barracks is its compact chapel, its adjacent yard having been opened up to the street during the supermarket conversion. This has revealed a fascinating group of headstones of long dead soldiers which have been cleaned up and re-positioned. Each tells a story of heroic deeds including fusiliers and dragoon guards who took part in battles such as Waterloo and the famous Charge of the Light Brigade.

55. The Birley Stone and Jaw Bone Hill
LANE HEAD, S30

High on a ridge, at the point where Lane Head rising out of Grenoside becomes Oughtibridge Lane which descends into the Don Valley, can be found the historic Birley Stone. Although precious little is known about it, ancient charters record that the stone has been standing here since 1161. It bears no inscription but may have served as some type of boundary stone. Adjacent is a recent stone bearing a plaque giving details of places visible from this excellent vantage point.

The ridge on which the stone stands is known oddly as Jaw Bone or Whalejaw Hill, which seems curious being so far from the sea. However, the name relates to a pair of whale's jaws which once formed a gateway to the road, so large that a cart of hay could be driven through them. It is said they were brought here as a souvenir by a Mr. Tingle who had made his fortune in the early days of the steel industry. The bones have long since rotted and been broken up.

56. An Argument Over Water
STORRS BRIDGE LANE, S6

Before the widespread production of steel, it was wrought iron, produced in blast furnaces, that was used for products such as armour plate, rails, wheels and axles. In the days before steam, wrought iron was made at water-powered forges dotted along Sheffield's many fast flowing rivers. Although little remains of these nineteenth century wrought iron works, the careful observer can still detect the man-made dams which turned the waterwheels to work the hammers. In the Loxley Valley can be found the Storrs Bridge Wheel dam begun in 1720, rebuilt after the Sheffield Flood of 1864 and worked until 1956. A curious stone lies in the undergrowth nearby inscribed "Mark Below, Two Feet Above Weir – As Agreed 1825". This recalls a dispute over water levels with the Loxley Old Wheel downstream, the dam of which also survives. It reminds us just how important a healthy flow of water was to a works in the days before steam.

The Charcoal Burner's Grave, Ecclesall Woods (see no. 34)

Further Reading:
South and West Yorkshire Curiosities (Duncan and Trevor Smith),
The Dovecote Press, 1992

Exploring Around South Yorkshire (Ian Dawson),
The Dovecote Press, 1994

The Odd, Amusing and Unusual in Sheffield (J. Edward Vickers),
Vickers, 1986

An Illustrated Guide to Sheffield (Pawson and Brailsford),
The Amethyst Press, 1862

An Architectural Trail of the Don Valley By Supertram,
The Sheffield Society of Architects, 1995

Acknowledgements:
Mel Humphreys (Noose & Gibbet, Attercliffe), Steve Hatton (Sheffield Bus Museum), Paul Billington, Simon Laffoley, Tim and Jane Hale, Mary Smith, Eva Holland and Joanne Jagiellowicz. Our thanks especially to Eleanor Waite for typing the manuscript.